For Jane

Enjoy Now!

What's **your** expiry date?

Embrace Your Mortality, Live with Vitality

Patrick Mathieu

Patrick Mathieu

UNLIMITED

Guelph, Ontario, Canada

Library and Archives Canada Cataloguing in Publication

Mathieu, Patrick, 1970-

What's your expiry date? : embrace your mortality, live with vitality / Patrick Mathieu.

ISBN 0-9738064-0-0

1. Self-actualization (Psychology)
2. Death—Psychological aspects.
3. Congenital heart disease—Patients—Canada—Biography.
4. Mathieu, Patrick, 1970- —Health. I. Title.

BF637.S4M415 2005 158.1
C2005-902883-1

ISBN 13: 978-09738064-0-3

Copies of *What's Your Expiry Date?* can be purchased for educational, business or promotional use. For information, please contact:
Patrick Mathieu Unlimited
48 Darling Crescent
Guelph, Ontario, Canada
N1L 1P8
booksales@mathieu.com

Editing: Jennifer Tribe, Juiced Consulting www.juicedconsulting.com

Cover Design, Interior Design and Layout: Sandy Peic,
Inspired Sight & Sound Inc. www.inspiredinc.ca

Author Photos: www.yanka.ca

Printed and bound in Canada by Friesens Corporation

For Benjamin Je t'aime, mon Ben!

Contents

Introduction

My Expiry Date

The Envelope _____ 5

A 'Bad' Heart _____ 7

The Meeting _____ 11

The Myth of Immortality

Denying Death _____ 19

Coming to Terms: My Journey Through

the Five Stages _____ 23

Stage One: Denial _____ 24

Stage Two: Anger _____ 27

Stage Three: Bargaining _____ 31

Stage Four: Depression _____ 33

Stage Five: Acceptance _____ 37

Embracing Mortality

Discovering a Sixth Stage _____ 43

Your Third Ghost _____ 47

Death on Your Terms _____ 50

Your Expiry Date _____ 54

Tapping into the Power of Mortality

The Mortality Manifesto _____ 61

The Mortality Manifesto Pledge _____ 63

The Past _____ 65

The Future _____ 73

The Present _____ 79

Dreams _____ 85

Fear _____ 88

Mindful Awareness _____ 94

Epilogue

About the Author

Acknowledgements

Mom and Dad – I'm not sure how you found the strength to make it through my first year of life. (Actually, I'm not sure how you made it through my teenage years either!) I can never thank you enough for giving me everything you could. I love you both very much.

Heather, my wife and my friend – When I said I was going to become a professional speaker, you believed in me. When I said I was going to write a book, you encouraged me. I love you, hun! Thanks for being the best co-pilot anyone could ask for.

Mike – You've taught me some very valuable lessons over the years. You continue to make me proud to call you my brother. I love you.

Allan, my dear friend, business manager, mentor, sounding board and above all, my magical librarian – You always know just when to lend me the perfect book that will expand my horizons and take me to the next level. Thanks for being in my corner.

Andy, my co-conspirator in so many of my life's adventures – I value your friendship and I'm so glad we continue to be a part of each other's lives.

Sr. Claire – You helped me become the communicator I am today.

My Mastermind Group (Carolyn, Dave, Jacques and Allan) – It's been great having your collective energy and input over the years. I hope I've been able to give back as much as I've received from our collaborations.

Toronto#1 Toastmasters – What a fantastic place to learn and grow. Thanks for allowing me to reconnect with what I love the most – speaking from the heart (pun intended) and touching people's souls.

Sandy, my graphic designer extraordinaire – You always do a fantastic job of taking my ideas and making them look great. I'm so glad you're part of my team.

Jennifer, my editor and guide through the publishing process – Your outstanding project management has made this painless, and your editing skills were invaluable.

Larry Hehn, Renate Zorn and Mike McGauley – Thanks for being kind enough to share your insights and experiences in the worlds of speaking and writing.

The Universe – We make a great team, don't we?

And thanks to everyone who, over the years, has approached me after a presentation to share a life story with me. First, thanks for opening up to someone you had only known for an hour or two. Second, thanks for letting me know I had touched you and helped you. Third, please know that you touched and helped me too.

Introduction

The story you are about to read revolves around a barcode I have tattooed on my right shoulder. In many ways, the story of this barcode is the story of my life so far.

In April 2003, I went for a massage. I was the last appointment of the day for Susan, my massage therapist, and I was certainly carrying all of the day's tensions with me in my back and shoulders.

Shortly after we started the session, Susan asked me about the barcode tattoo on my shoulder. Although she had treated me on previous visits, the topic of my tattoo had never come up. I decided to tell her what it means and why I felt compelled to have it put there.

Over the course of our hour-long session, I told Susan the story you are about to read. It certainly wasn't the first time I had told this story, but up to that point, I had only shared this personal account with very close friends.

When our session concluded, she smiled a big smile at me and said:

"You know, that's an incredible story. Even though it's the end of a long day, I feel totally energized and motivated. I want to *do* something! You've really inspired me."

At the time, I just laughed and told her I was glad to help her as much as she had helped me. However, over the next few weeks her comments began to replay over and over again in my mind. It felt really good to motivate and inspire someone simply by relating my experiences.

Then it dawned on me. If I could motivate one person with this story by telling it while half-naked, lying on a table with my face in a hole, imagine how many people I could help if I began to share my story with others in a more professional manner!

And that's why you have this book in your hands. I only hope you get as much out of my story as Susan did.

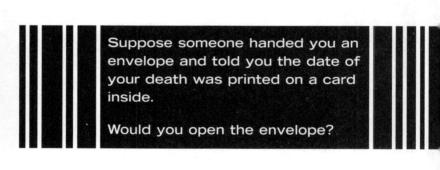

Suppose someone handed you an envelope and told you the date of your death was printed on a card inside.

Would you open the envelope?

The Envelope

Do you know when you're going to die?

If you could find out, would you?

Suppose someone handed you an envelope and told you the date of your death was printed on a card inside. Would you open the envelope?

More importantly, if you did open it, what would you do differently? How would you change the way you live your life?

I have news for you. **The book you're holding in your hands right now is that envelope.**

I've written this book in the hopes that I can help you begin thinking seriously about what's truly important to you and about how you're living your life.

My goal is to motivate you to live your life on purpose and to make better decisions. I'm going to share lessons that, if you take them to heart, will allow you to conquer fear and doubt and to live with certainty. I want to bring you to the point where if someone were to ask what you would do differently if you knew the date of your death, you'd be able to smile and say, **"Not a thing**."

What qualifies me to help you in these ways?

I'm lucky enough to know the day I'm going to die.

This is my expiry date:

A 'Bad' Heart

I was born with a 'bad' heart. It was just made wrong. In fact, I've had leading cardiologists tell me that if they were to build a heart the way mine is built, it would never run.

On paper, the doctors classify it as 'complex cardiac anatomy' and the detailed medical description continues for four paragraphs. I'll spare you the full medical details, but I do want to give you a graphic example of one aspect of my problem.

I have a very large hole in the wall between the two lower chambers of my heart. This is called a Ventricular Septal Defect, and by itself, it's not uncommon. What makes mine unusual is the size of the hole.

I recently had a full MRI (Magnetic Resonance Imaging) scan done of my heart. The scan revealed that the hole in my heart is 1.4 inches by 1.3 inches. When I read that fact in my medical report, I was shocked.

I cut out a piece of black paper that is 1.4 inches by 1.3 inches. Since a person's heart is roughly the size of his or her fist, I photographed my fist with the paper 'hole.' Have a look on the next page.

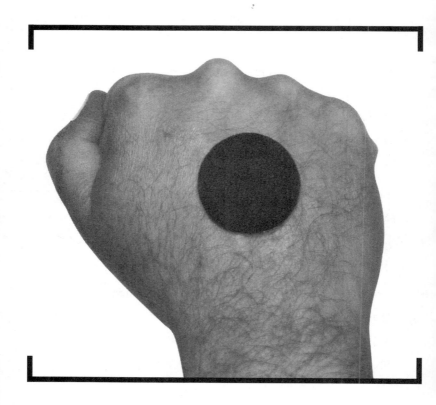

At birth, the doctors discovered the extent of my congenital heart disease and told my parents I probably wouldn't make it through my first year. I spent a lot of that first year sick and in the hospital. I can't imagine what my poor parents had to endure during that time, not knowing if their first-born child would survive. *(Mom and Dad—thanks for everything.)*

Much to the amazement of the doctors and nurses, I survived that first year and my condition stabilized. They performed more diagnostic tests on me in an effort to discover exactly why my heart continued to work when medical science told them it shouldn't be working at all.

Ultimately, they decided not to tamper with my heart unless they needed to, and since there have never been any complications, I've never had any surgery on my heart.

Growing up, I was never aware of my heart problem— except when I ran. I would get tired *much* faster than the other kids. Also, I would go for an annual checkup with the cardiology team at the nearby children's hospital. Each year, I presented myself at the hospital and spent the better part of the day with my shirt off for X-rays, electrocardiograms and various other tests.

As the years passed, the tests became more sophisticated, however, the results were always the same: total disbelief and amazement on the part of the medical professionals. To tell you the truth, I really enjoyed that part. It made me feel good to stump the experts!

I was fortunate enough to have a wonderful cardiologist who told me year after year that there was a very special balance at work in my life. He explained that I had a number of conditions that somehow balanced one another and kept me going. But I wasn't just going—I was thriving.

As amazed as the people at the children's hospital were at my heart condition, they were equally puzzled that I was consistently far above average for height and weight in my age category. With my complex condition they expected me to be a scrawny, underdeveloped boy. This wouldn't be the last time medical science would underestimate me.

The Meeting

When I turned 18, I was no longer eligible to be treated at the children's hospital, so I was sent to a very prestigious heart institute. I was really looking forward to my first visit. I was eager to hear what this new team of experts would say about my unusual condition.

After a battery of tests, I finally met with one of the cardiologists who specialized in adults with congenital heart conditions.

This meeting altered the course of my life.

When I entered the doctor's office, I noticed a very thick file on his desk. After I sat down, he patted the file and told me he had reviewed all of my records and information that the children's hospital had sent over. He also told me he had reviewed all of the tests that had been conducted at the heart institute. And finally, he assured me that all of this information had been reviewed by an entire team of doctors, including the top heart surgeon in the country. He went so far as to show me their signatures on the report.

Then, with great matter-of-factness, he told me there was nothing they could do for me. His comment sent a chill down my spine. I had always enjoyed stumping the experts, but suddenly this didn't seem right.

There's nothing we can do for you.

Nothing you can do for me?

Why would I need someone to *do* anything?

What needed *doing*?

At the children's hospital, their disbelief and amazement were always followed up with the stern warning to pay attention to what my body was telling me and to stop any activity that was causing me concern. They always reassured me, and my parents, that I was the best judge of my capabilities. Now I was being told there was nothing the top team in Canada could do for me. Clearly, something had changed.

This doctor went on to explain that since they didn't understand why my heart was beating successfully, there was nothing they could do to fix it. He also told me a transplant was out of the question.

A heart transplant??

My mind raced.

Why would I need a heart transplant?

I had been living the normal life of an 18-year-old. I had no symptoms. No pain. This was supposed to be just a routine checkup and now he was talking about a heart transplant?

At this point in the consultation, it seemed as though time itself slowed down. The entire room seemed to fade away until it was just me and the doctor, sitting alone in outer space. He began to explain something to me in words I can never forget. It didn't sound like a doctor talking to an 18-year-old patient; it sounded like a medical professor talking to a group of medical students.

"The heart is a muscle," he began. "Like any muscle, it will give out over time. Because of the physiology of your

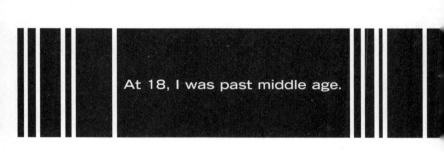

At 18, I was past middle age.

heart, it will give out much sooner. We hope that doesn't happen until you are 30 or so."

I said nothing.

He said nothing.

Finally I asked him, "Let me get this straight—you *HOPE* that I live to be *30?*"

"Yes," was his answer.

You *HOPE* that I live to be *30?*

Yes.

I don't remember much more of the conversation. About a week later, it finally sunk in that my life was more than half over. At 18, I was past middle age.

Imagine getting that news. Think how that would affect your life.

In time, I came to realize this news was the greatest gift I'd ever been given—but I certainly didn't feel that way at first.

As you can imagine, coming to terms with this news took a long time. What I want to share with you now is the thought process I went through, the lessons I learned and the incredible excitement I have as a result. Furthermore, I want to show you how to apply these lessons to improve your own life—*today*.

The Myth of
Immortality

"The idea of death, the fear of it, haunts the human animal like nothing else; it is a mainspring of human activity—activity designed largely to avoid the fatality of death, to overcome it by denying in some way that it is the final destiny..."

Ernest Becker in *The Denial of Death*

Denying Death

We work very hard to convince ourselves we are immortal. Many industries have sprung up to aid and abet us in this delusion. Cosmetics make promises about reversing the effects of aging. If that doesn't work, there's always cosmetic surgery. Medicine, whose objective of improving the *quality* of life is often confused with improving the *quantity* of life, constantly struggles to push back life expectancy dates. Supplements, diets, exercise regimens, miracle foods, the list goes on and on. Like Ponce de León, we're all involved in our own search for the fountain of youth.

In today's Western society, people don't die anymore. They pass on, pass away, cross over, pass over, transition or return home. We don't talk about dead people. We speak of the dearly departed or the deceased.

I've had long discussions with people who disagree that we actively deny death. Often people will point to the success of books like *Tuesdays With Morrie* by Mitch Albom or television shows like HBO's *Six Feet Under*.

While I admit that, at times, we can have a fascination with death, this is very different from a healthy acceptance of death as a fact of life. In *Tuesdays With Morrie*, we read about a man who watches a friend die. The reader is twice removed from the actual experience of death!

Death is the great equalizer. Everyone dies. And yet, very few people voluntarily give death any serious thought.

When parents are expecting a new child, there are countless resources available: books, videos, training classes, special accessories. There's an entire industry devoted to being born and we find it perfectly natural to immerse ourselves in the preparation for what's about to come.

Why, then, don't we do the same for death? Why isn't there a death industry complete with books, videos and training classes?

Let me be clear that I'm not talking about resources to help people cope with the loss of others. I'm also not talking about the funeral care business. I'm talking about a support system to help people acknowledge and prepare as early as possible for the inevitability of their own death.

Just think how powerful you would be if you were able to live your entire life without the fear of death.

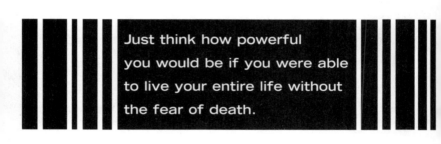

Just think how powerful
you would be if you were able
to live your entire life without
the fear of death.

Coming to Terms: My Journey Through the Five Stages

In her landmark book, *On Death and Dying*, Dr. Elisabeth Kübler-Ross discussed lessons learned by interviewing and working with over 200 dying patients in the late 1960s. Through this experience, she identified five stages that most dying people go through: denial, anger, bargaining, depression and acceptance.

I want to stress that the merits of the Five Stages model have been greatly debated and there are certainly alternate theories. Furthermore, Kübler-Ross herself revised her position on the matter in later years. However, I find the five stages to be a useful starting place for the discussion of my experience.

Kübler-Ross described these stages as coping mechanisms used by people to help them adjust to the reality of dying. As you'll see from my own experience, there isn't necessarily a clear progression from one stage to another and it's possible to be in more than one stage at the same time. It's also possible that some people spend little or no time at all in some of the stages.

Stage One: Denial

> *"Since in our unconscious mind we are all immortal, it is almost inconceivable for us to acknowledge that we too have to face death."*
>
> **Dr. Elisabeth Kübler-Ross** in *On Death and Dying*

When confronted with one's own mortality, the first stage is often denial. Kübler-Ross describes patients 'shopping around' for second, third and fourth opinions.

I certainly had a good number of friends and family members who told me I should be getting a second opinion. "Clearly, this doctor missed something," they'd say. "Look at you! You look fine to me. He must be wrong."

I must confess, the temptation to live in denial was strong, but ultimately, my denial period was short-lived for three main reasons.

First, when my care was being transferred to the adult heart institute I was filled with excitement at the prospect of having the pre-eminent specialists in the land working with me. This was one of the top cardiology facilities in the country. How could I now cast doubt on their prognosis just because I didn't like it?

Canada's top heart surgeon had signed off on my file. The scientific evidence was very powerful. It was as if I'd already had a ruling from the Supreme Court. Where do you go to appeal?

Second, it wasn't as if I didn't know about my heart condition. Many of the patients involved in Kübler-Ross' research were facing their mortality as a result of a recent diagnosis of cancer or other terminal illness. I had been living with my condition all my life. The only new information this doctor had for me was when the story was going to end.

Third, I saw no logical reason to seek another opinion. In my mind, seeking a second opinion was a fool's game. After all, if the first doctor could be wrong, what assurance was there that the second or third doctor wouldn't also be wrong? Furthermore, what if the second opinion turned out to be worse than the first? What if the second doctor's prognosis was for a 25-year life expectancy?

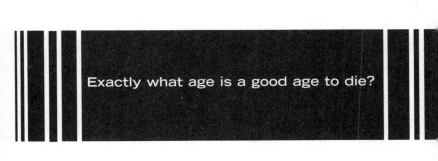

Exactly what age is a good age to die?

I asked myself if I'd feel better if the prediction was for 35 or 40 years of life. This brought up a very interesting self-dialogue:

"Exactly what age is a good age to die?"

"Hmm... I think 80 is a good age."

"Eighty? Are you sure? Let me ask you again when you're 79."

The one thing I knew for sure, 30 was *far* too young! This moved me quickly into the second stage: anger.

Stage Two: Anger

"When the first stage of denial cannot be maintained any longer, it is replaced by feelings of anger, rage, envy and resentment. The next logical question becomes, "Why me?"

Dr. Elisabeth Kübler-Ross in *On Death and Dying*

When I entered the 'why me' stage, everything and everyone became a focal point for my anger.

A good deal of anger was directed at my father. He had a series of medical conditions that, in my mind, were self-inflicted. He was a lifelong smoker. He never exercised and was overweight. He had recently developed adult-onset diabetes and I attributed this to his weight and poor eating habits.

My anger at my father came from two places. First, because I loved my father and didn't want to see anything bad happen to him, I was angry that he wasn't respecting himself (or his family) enough to take things seriously. Second, his doctor constantly gave him steps he could take to start turning things around (stop smoking, eat right, get regular exercise) and yet he chose not to follow these steps.

I, on the other hand, wasn't given any steps to turn things around. There was nothing I could do, or stop doing, that would change my situation. My lack of options brought about feelings of helplessness, which manifested as anger.

I was also angry with my peers. They were typical teenagers. They weren't sure what they were going to do with their lives and they weren't worried about it.

They had all the time in the world, while I had about 12 more years to live. I felt they were taking everything for granted, and I became upset with them for not realizing what they had.

Back at school, one of my friends had started a suicide prevention group and he asked me to show my support by attending their first meeting. At this point, I still hadn't told many people about my news, and as I sat there and listened to my fellow students complain about the issues that were driving them to consider taking their own lives, I became enraged.

"You people need a kick in the ass!" I blurted out. Being completely insensitive, I went on to lecture all of them, including the faculty advisor, on what a *real* problem was.

I told them what I was facing and asked them if they thought their situations were better or worse than mine. I then chastised each of them for even thinking of throwing away something that I was trying desperately to hold onto.

My anger was constantly fueled by the 'why me' question. Lying in my bed at night, I would wonder, over and over, why I'd been given this horribly cruel fate.

I remember thinking that if I had to die young, why would the universe wait until I'm 30? Why not take me at 10 or five? By the time I made it to 30, I'd just be starting to settle into a life of my own and beginning to make plans for the future.

Thoughts about the future were one of the most upsetting things because I'd find myself daydreaming about having a career or a wife or about what I'd look like when I was 95. Then reality would come crashing back on me and I'd be angry again.

As you'll soon see, my anger stage overlapped with my depression stage. However, over a period of months I began to make peace with my situation. I'm so thankful I was able to work through my anger at my father well before he eventually died in May 2000.

In time, I came up with an answer to the constant question of 'why me.'

The answer was surprisingly simple:

Because you're human and *everyone* dies.

Stage Three: Bargaining

"The bargaining is really an attempt to postpone..."

Dr. Elisabeth Kübler-Ross in *On Death and Dying*

Initially, my bargaining was expressed as the resurfacing of a dialogue from my denial stage.

"Thirty is too young. It's too soon.
Give me more time!"

And, as in the denial stage, two questions kept coming back.

"How long is long enough?
What age is a good age to die?"

In my case, I didn't enter too deeply into bargaining. I kept bumping up against the logic of the 'what age is a good age to die' question.

My bargaining manifested itself as an unspoken gesture: I began to hit the gym. I secretly hoped that if I whipped my body into better shape, I could squeeze a few more years out of it. Somehow, God would see that I was actually doing my part to take care of myself and I would be granted a stay of execution.

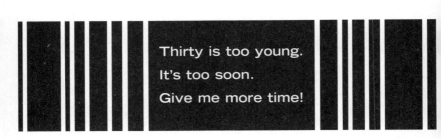

Thirty is too young.
It's too soon.
Give me more time!

Stage Four: Depression

> *"What we often tend to forget, however, is the preparatory grief that the terminally ill patient has to undergo in order to prepare himself for his final separation from this world."*

Dr. Elisabeth Kübler-Ross in *On Death and Dying*

Kübler-Ross described two kinds of depression that can be faced by the terminally ill: reactive depression and preparatory depression.

Reactive depression is in reaction to a loss that has occurred, such as the loss of mobility, the loss of bodily control, the loss of hair due to treatments, the loss of a breast.

In my case, I had suffered no loss, endured no surgery and felt no different, so I didn't experience reactive depression. My depression was all preparatory.

Preparatory depression, Kübler-Ross maintained, is a necessary step on the road to acceptance. Rather than being caused by past losses, this type of depression deals with impending losses.

I had just been accepted as a student at the very prestigious McGill University in Montreal. Before my visit with the cardiologist, I was excited at the prospect of attending McGill. It was something I had worked for four years to achieve.

The expiry date changed all that. I no longer wanted to go to school. I only had 12 years left to live and I became very depressed at the thought of 'wasting' a third of that time in university, studying for a career I'd never live to have.

Ultimately, I did go to university, and I remember filling out the forms for my student loan. I was laughing so hard because the terms of the loan called for me to finish repaying when I was almost 34. I took great satisfaction in knowing the bank would never get all of its money back.

At the time I received my expiry date, I didn't have a steady girlfriend and I began to seriously doubt I ever would. After all, who would want to get emotionally involved with someone who had 12 years to live? This was a tremendous source of anguish for me.

All my life, I had pictured myself with a wife and children. The most important thing I could imagine doing was raising a child to be a good member of society. I believe that's how you leave a legacy—not by how much money you earn, or how many buildings you own, but by the quality of the people you leave behind to continue on.

Now my dream was shattered. I became convinced no one would want to get emotionally involved with me. Even on the off-chance someone did, there was no responsible way I could bring a child into the world.

I was constantly haunted by an image. It was a cold, gray, rainy day. A crying woman, holding a newborn baby, was standing at a graveside. My name was on the headstone.

> How could I do that to anyone? How could I ruin two lives like that? How selfish would that be?

This recurring image brought about alternating feelings of depression and anger. The anger revolved around the 'why me' question again.

Why shouldn't I be allowed to experience love?

Does this mean I'm just supposed to go off to a mountain top and wait to die?

Why should I cut myself off from any possibility of love and happiness?

Surely I deserve love and happiness as much as anyone else.

I found myself in a vicious cycle. I'd get angry at the situation that was creating the impending loss, then, once the sense of loss overwhelmed me, I'd get depressed at the complete lack of options. My lack of options would feed the 'why me' question, and I'd start all over again.

Stage Five: Acceptance

"If a patient has had enough time...he will reach a stage during which he is neither depressed nor angry about his 'fate.'"

Dr. Elisabeth Kübler-Ross in *On Death and Dying*

My experience with the acceptance stage was markedly different from the experience of Kübler-Ross' patients. That's because my fifth stage was immediately followed by the realization that there's one more stage.

My acceptance came about through another series of internal dialogues.

> **"Well, I'm going to die."**

> "You and everyone else. You're no different."

> **"But I know when to expect it."**

> **"Hey, that's kind of exciting! Most people are oblivious until it's too late. I can actually *do* something with that knowledge."**

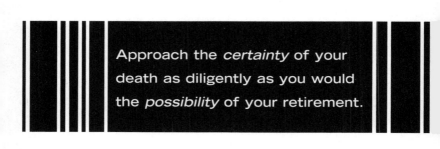

Approach the *certainty* of your death as diligently as you would the *possibility* of your retirement.

I began to realize that most people live their lives as if they're immortal, and yet they're obviously not. Sooner or later, their mortality catches up with them and it's often too late to make any changes.

My acceptance of death, and the realization that there is a sixth stage of coming to terms with mortality, came to me as soon as I made a critical distinction. Nobody knows when he or she will die—*but I knew*! I wasn't given a death sentence; I was given an early wake-up call! I was allowed to peek ahead and see what came next.

In her book, Kübler-Ross maintained that "acceptance should not be mistaken for a happy stage. It is almost always devoid of feelings."

How very sad.

I think Kübler-Ross encountered a lack of feeling in patients in the acceptance stage because she was dealing with people who were coming to terms with their mortality at the end of their lives. I discovered the sixth stage— what I call the Power of Mortality—because I came to terms with my death well before I was expected to die.

I wasn't sick. I wasn't in pain or suffering. I felt fine. For me, that distinction made all the difference in the world.

You see, it's never a question of *if* we're going to die, but only a question of *when*.

People who are just entering the workforce will often set up retirement savings plans even though retirement may be 40 or 50 years away. Why? Because they know that if they live long enough, they'll retire and they'll need to be financially ready for that possibility.

What I'm advocating is that you approach the *certainty* of your death as diligently as you would the *possibility* of your retirement.

From a solid foundation of acceptance, you're ready to move from the fear-filled world of the immortals to the exciting and joy-filled world of the mortals.

Let me show you how.

Discovering a Sixth Stage

Six years after my fateful meeting with that cardiologist, I finally reached what I call the sixth stage: the Power of Mortality. It had been a long and often difficult journey, but I had moved beyond simple acceptance and into the excitement and power that came from embracing my own mortality.

To mark this important transition, in fact to celebrate that transition, I planned a very personal and private ceremony. Since this book has been all about sharing my personal and private story with you, I'll now relate the details of that ceremony.

The date was April 15, 1994. I was living in Montreal. I set my alarm clock to waken me very, very early in the morning. I brewed a pot of coffee and poured it into a thermos. I put the thermos and my camera into my backpack. I dressed warmly and began to walk through the dark, up the winding trails, to the top of Mount Royal.

Once I reached the top, I made my way to the beautiful scenic lookout that faces south but offers an incredible view of the south, east and west. I poured myself some coffee and sat in the dark reviewing the last six years.

I thought about my appointment with the cardiologist and all of the lows and highs that had followed. I cried for my lost innocence. I thought about what I had learned and how I had changed as a result of my new knowledge. I thought about what might lay ahead. Then, I simply enjoyed my coffee and waited for the sun to rise.

When the sun finally broke free of the horizon, I took a deep breath and rejoiced. I made a solemn vow that I wouldn't take that day for granted. I told myself that April 15, 1994 was my new birthday and the day of my death all in one. I vowed that if I lived to see April 16, 1994, I wouldn't take that day for granted either—or any of the others that may follow, regardless of how many there might be.

I will always treasure the photo I took of that sunrise. The morning sun broke over the horizon of the distant hills and lit up the mist over the St. Lawrence River, silhouetting the office towers of downtown Montreal. In the years since, I've often drawn strength and serenity from that photo. You can see it for yourself at http://www.mathieu.com/newday.html.

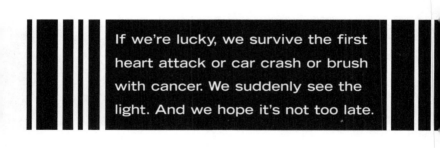

If we're lucky, we survive the first heart attack or car crash or brush with cancer. We suddenly see the light. And we hope it's not too late.

Your Third Ghost

Everyone faces death. There's nothing any of us can do to avoid it. Nothing changes it—not economic status or social standing, not education or ethnicity or nationality or gender. None of it matters when it comes to death. It truly is the great equalizer.

Upon reaching the sixth stage of facing my mortality, I felt like I'd been let in on a huge secret. It was as though I could see everyone else wearing a blindfold, groping through life, hoping that somehow everything would work out.

Some people move very slowly while wearing these blindfolds, tentatively feeling their way around, afraid to bump into anything or anyone. Some people charge headlong in any given direction, not wanting to appear unsure of themselves. Others simply hang on to someone else and trust that person knows where to go.

By and large though, no one stops to think about the big picture; no one is willing to admit that, sooner or later, death will come. A blindfold fools you into thinking you're immortal.

Having had my blindfold forcibly removed, I could clearly see I was mortal. My mortality gave me tremendous joy and power.

If you're familiar with Charles Dickens' *A Christmas Carol*, you'll recall that Ebenezer Scrooge doesn't decide to change his ways until the third ghost brings him face to face with his own grave. Isn't that a common theme in our society?

We rush through life making mountains out of our daily molehills. There are reports to write, meetings to attend, calls to make, a corporate ladder to climb. We work to be able to afford all of the 'toys' that we buy to distract ourselves from the fact that we spend all of our time work-ing. We scramble from one crisis to another, all the while forgetting about the big picture.

Then, if we're lucky, we survive the first heart attack or car crash or brush with cancer. We suddenly see the light. Like Scrooge, once we see our own graves, we change our ways and make peace with our world. And we hope it's not too late.

Imagine if everyone could reach that point of peace without having to undergo a traumatic experience? Wouldn't it be great if we could work through the stages of dying while we're still healthy and while we still have time to make changes?

I'm here to act as your own personal 'third ghost.' I'm showing you your grave and I'm trying to gently remove your blindfold. I'm inviting you to join me in the exciting world of the mortals.

Death on Your Terms

Perhaps you have no desire to acknowledge your own death. Why would anyone want to put him- or herself through the process of coming to terms with death? After all, ignorance is bliss. If we're living healthy and happy lives, who wants to think about death? Why not simply continue merrily along until the Grim Reaper knocks on the door?

My answer to that can be found in a quote from Paulo Coelho in his book *The Alchemist*:

> *So why is it so important to live our personal calling if we are only going to suffer more than other people?*
>
> *Because, once we have overcome the defeats—and we always do—we are filled by a greater sense of euphoria and confidence. In the silence of our hearts, we know that we are proving ourselves worthy of the miracle of life. Each day, each hour, is part of the good fight. We start to live with enthusiasm and pleasure. Intense, unexpected suffering passes more quickly than suffering that is apparently bearable; the latter goes on for years and, without our noticing, eats away at our soul, until, one day, we are no longer able to free ourselves from the bitterness and it stays with us for the rest of our lives.*

The implications of our inability or unwillingness to acknowledge and come to terms with mortality extend beyond our own death to include the death of others. We don't want to think about ourselves dying and we don't want to think about others dying either. In some cases, the death of another can be a debilitating loss because we're totally unprepared. In other cases, the death of another disturbs us because it's a subconscious reminder of our own ticking clock.

In 2004, I spoke at the national convention for the Funeral Service Association of Canada. After my presentation, I chatted with a number of funeral service professionals. They told me the single most troubling issue for bereaved families is the fact that they didn't have enough time with the deceased. Perhaps they didn't get a chance to say good-bye or to say a final "I love you."

If we don't acknowledge death, we run the risk of moving through life always assuming that there will be enough time. Time to do things that haven't been done. Time to say things that haven't been said. Time to right wrongs and heal wounds.

If we don't acknowledge death,
we run the risk of moving through
life always assuming that there will
be enough time.

I'm encouraging you to embrace your mortality because I want you to live with the peace that comes from knowing that when a loved one dies, you won't have to suffer the terrible fate of having left something unsaid or undone.

Whether we accept it or not, whether we acknowledge it or not, we all have to face death. When death taps us on the shoulder, we can't ignore the call.

I encourage you to come to terms with your own death as soon as possible—the earlier the better. Because isn't it better to face death on your own terms rather than cancer's terms? Or the heart attack's terms? Or the car accident's terms?

Your Expiry Date

Now we've reached a critical point. In each of my keynote speeches and seminars, I challenge my audience members to make a leap of faith. I have to issue the same challenge to you right now. The information that follows this point in the book has the potential to change your life forever—but only if you approach it from the proper perspective.

What I need you to do right now is acknowledge your mortality.

If the idea of acknowledging your own death still terrifies you, please put this book down. You can come back to it later. But to read further, you need to acknowledge your mortality. Please note that I don't expect you to *accept* your death, merely acknowledge it. As I can attest, acceptance can be a long process.

I've come to realize the power of accepting mortality because I was forced to acknowledge and accept my death at an early age. I had no choice. I was told when I was going to die. So far, you probably haven't had to make that adjustment because you haven't been told when you will die.

Well, my friend, if you're willing to move forward, let's agree that *today* is the day you die.

This is it! This is your final day.

Be assured that I'm not trying to be morbid, nor am I trying to be sensationalistic. The fact of the matter is that while you probably won't die today, *no one* on earth can make that guarantee. None of us has any certainty when it comes to life and death. The only thing we can be certain about is right now.

That makes now a pretty powerful moment, doesn't it?

I'm urging you to acknowledge that life is uncertain, and that no one owes you any more time than you've already been given. I want to give you your own personal expiry date.

At the back of this book, you'll find a page with your very own barcode on it. Please turn to that page and write today's date on the line under the barcode.

Acknowledge your mortality. While you probably won't die today, *no one* on earth can make that guarantee.

Next, I suggest you photocopy the page and keep it with you to remind you that *now* is the only time of which you are certain. Whenever you look at your barcode, you'll remember that today could very well have been your last day. Each day since then has been a bonus and a gift.

You might want to make multiple copies of your barcode and keep one at work, one on your bathroom mirror and one in the car. And here's something that I find quite powerful: keep a copy with your checkbook. If you're ever worrying about your finances, seeing that barcode helps put things in perspective in a hurry.

Once you agree that today is the day you'll die, something amazing happens. If you wake up tomorrow morning, the world will look quite different. Actually, the world will be the same, but *you* will be changed.

Without your blindfold, you'll see with the eyes of some- one who realizes what a gift you've been given. You've been given the gift of *now*. And if you wake up the next day, you'll really begin to appreciate what you have. If you're doing it right, the feeling intensifies each day, as does the sense of power and vitality that's provided by living life as a mortal.

Before proceeding, it's absolutely essential that you acknowledge you aren't owed any specific amount of time. What follows next has the most impact if you've made this distinction.

Ready?

Tapping into the
Power of Mortality

The Mortality Manifesto

In science fiction, immortality is often depicted as the ultimate super power. I maintain that embracing your **mortality** gives you the ultimate power: the power to choose what kind of life you want to live. The best part is that it's a choice you get to make over and over again, on a daily basis.

Almost everyone I meet lives as though he or she is immortal. People always assume there will be 'more time.' Even more dangerously, they assume there will be 'enough time.'

- Enough time to do the things that haven't been done.

- Enough time to say the things that haven't been said.

- Enough time to right wrongs and heal wounds.

- Enough time to follow their true path.

- Enough time to live their life!

I challenge you to accept your mortality. You don't need to know when you're going to die; you just have to accept that you will die.

Let me say that again.

You... will... die.

The sooner you accept and come to terms with your own mortality, the sooner you free yourself from the illusion of unlimited time and allow yourself to start living your life on purpose. You begin to harness the power of each moment and treasure 'now' for the gift it truly is.

Join me in the exciting world of the all-powerful mortals, won't you? If you're up for it, take the Mortality Manifesto Pledge on the next page.

Mortality Manifesto Pledge

My name is _____ .

I was born. I will die.

I accept this. I embrace it.

I do not dwell on the past, nor do I waste time worrying about the future.

I use each moment to the fullest.

I always strive to ensure that my every thought, word and action is moving me in the direction of my dreams.

Because fear is based on an imagined future, my focus on the present makes me fearless.

Accepting my mortality allows me to live a life full of vitality and power!

A life filled with joy!

A life with no regrets!

This is the gift I give to myself – today and every day!

Date: _____

Signed: _____

Let's examine the Mortality Manifesto's key components one by one so you can see exactly what the Power of Mortality is all about.

If you want to go even deeper into the principles behind the Mortality Manifesto, you'll want to have a copy of *The Mortality Manual*, the companion workbook to this book. The workbook offers a range of exercises to help you accept your mortality so that you can uncover and live your true dreams.

You can find out more about *The Mortality Manual* on my web site at http://www.mathieu.com.

The Past

I do not dwell on the past...

Why do some people have a tendency to become stuck in the past? When it comes to living in the past, there are two major variations on the theme.

First, there are those who constantly relive past glories or accomplishments. These people define themselves by who they were and what they did. These people believe that who they were in the past is who they will be in the future. Or that what they've had in the past is what they will have in the future.

When life takes an unexpected twist, people who live in the past often have a very difficult time adjusting because they're too busy living in a state of disbelief.

"This sort of thing doesn't happen to me."

"I never expected this."

"How can this be happening?"

"How will I ever cope?"

So far, scientists have said time travel is impossible. Yet I know someone who does it on a regular basis.

We probably all know people who've said or thought these things.

The second group is made up of those who constantly relive past setbacks or failures, and who define themselves by the problems they've had in the past. Strangely enough, these people, like the first group, also believe that who they were in the past is who they will be in the future. They let the shadows of the past keep them from achieving wonderful things in the present.

These shadows often obscure the new opportunities and possibilities that life is constantly offering them in the present.

> "I've never had any luck."

> "The world is out to get me."

> "Why would things get better now?"

> "Why bother trying?"

Again, we probably all know people who've said or thought these things.

So far, scientists have said time travel is impossible. Yet I know someone who does it on a regular basis. If the wrong name is mentioned or a painful subject is raised, this person is able, in the blink of an eye, to transport himself back to the moment when the pain and anger were fresh. His entire demeanor changes and it's as though he's right there, reliving the entire event. He can instantly ruin a great mood in the present just by thinking of some issues that are long past.

Living with a focus on the past leads to playing the 'if only' game. Those who had negative experiences in the past will say things such as:

> "If only I had said something differently,
> she'd still be with me now."

> "If only my boss had given me a break."

> "If only I hadn't bought that car."

Those who had positive experiences in the past will say things such as:

> "If only things were as good as they were then."

"If only I could run as fast as I used to."

"If only I still had my hair."

By law, investment companies must use a disclaimer stating that past performance should not be taken as an indication of future performance. There's a good reason for this disclaimer. The past can give us clues and teach us important lessons, but it can't be used to predict the future.

The problem with focusing on the past is that it can't change anything. Imagine you're watching a sporting event. If the player misses the goal, you can bet she won't score on the instant replay either. Nothing any of us does will change the past; dwelling on it only leads to self-destructive feelings. One of the most damaging self-destructive feelings is regret.

Let me give you a very personal example. My father was a man filled with humor. He was the life of the party and always had 10 jokes ready for any given occasion. His stories were legendary. To this day, I have friends who still talk about stories my dad first told them more than 20 years ago.

Hang on to the lessons
and let go of the circumstances
that brought them to you.

On numerous occasions, I heard people say to him, "You missed your calling. You should have been a comedian."

Whenever someone would say that, a cloud would pass over my dad's face for just a second. I could tell deep in his heart, he always wondered, "What if?"

How often does that happen to us? How often have we thought about some long-forgotten passion of ours and wondered, "What if?" How often have we had others tell us we missed our calling? What a horrible situation in which to find ourselves.

My goal, both for myself and for you, is to never have that cloud of deep regret pass over our faces. I want to ensure you never look back at your life and wish you had done things differently. I want to help you remove 'what if' and 'if only' from your vocabulary.

I'm fortunate enough to have inherited my father's sense of humor. Growing up, people used to say to me, "Oh, you're just like your father! You should be a comedian."

After receiving my expiry date and coming to terms with

my own mortality, I was adamant I wouldn't live with regrets. So I put together a routine and went to a local comedy club in Montreal for their amateur night.

It was great. Absolutely fantastic. That summer, I did three shows at the club—and realized that, although I enjoy performing and making people laugh, comedy as a career just isn't for me. The important thing is that I tried it. Now I know I'll never have any regrets in that area.

That's the gift I want to give you. I want you to live as a mortal. I want you to have the presence of mind to see the opportunities before you, the courage to explore them and the peace of mind that follows. You'll know you gave life your best and you'll have no regrets.

I certainly don't think the past is of no importance or has nothing to teach us. The Mortality Manifesto specifically says, "I do not *dwell* on the past." The use of the word 'dwell' acknowledges that the past holds lessons for us. What we need to do, however, is hang on to the lessons and let go of the circumstances that brought them to us.

The Future

... nor do I waste time worrying about the future.

Everyone looks to the future. Western society is constantly pushing us to plan for the future and to set goals and objectives. I know many people who have a five-year plan for themselves. I see no problem with this kind of thinking as long as two conditions are met.

First, any long-term plan needs a good amount of flexibility. Circumstances change frequently and you need to be able to adapt. You need to understand the difference between objectives and details.

I've met a number of forward-thinking people who believe they must concern themselves with the details in order to set objectives. They can tell you exactly how their life is going to unfold. They have every single detail planned out in advance. However, if one of those details doesn't work out as planned, they often feel the entire situation is hopeless.

Many people spend so much time thinking about the future, they forget that the only way to get there is through a series of todays.

Since there can be many routes to the same destination, meticulous planning only works if you have control over all of the details. Be careful not to delude yourself into thinking you can develop contingency plans for every possible situation. I can personally attest that life has a way of proving you wrong.

The second condition for forward thinking is that proper attention must be paid to the present. Many people spend so much time thinking about the future, they forget that the only way to get there is through a series of todays. These are the people who dream about being wealthy in the future, yet spend more than they earn in the present. I'll speak more about this in the section on the present.

Worry is nothing more than a useless waste of energy. Let me explain. Worry comes from imagining what may or may not come to pass. For most people, worrying is a natural part of life, because most people are attempting to live their lives in the future rather than in the present.

I want to be clear: Future-based goals and objectives are good and necessary, as long as they're kept in perspective.

But if they become our sole focus, we miss out on the gifts the present brings.

We can be so goal-oriented that we don't take time to appreciate what we've already achieved. Consider a dieter who obsesses so much over losing the last five pounds that he forgets to rejoice over how much he's already lost.

Placing too much focus on the future can lead you into something I call the Once Trap. I'm sure you're familiar with this trap; there are two versions of it.

People caught in the first version of the Once Trap are constantly saying there will be time for their goals and dreams once something happens.

> "I'll finally travel around the world once I make senior partner."

> "I'll start my own business once I finish my MBA."

> "I'll get involved in local theater once the kids move out."

People stuck in this version of the Once Trap run the risk of never starting anything because they're waiting for something else to happen first. Of course, looking at these situations as a mortal, you realize that an even deeper danger is being unhappy with yourself if you don't make it to the end of those situations. What if you die without ever traveling the world, starting your own business or acting in local theater?

The second version of the Once Trap has people living in a self-imposed state of purgatory by delaying their happiness until some future date.

> "All of my hard work will have paid off once I have $10,000 cash in the bank."

> "I'll find true love once I get my weight down to 150 pounds."

> "I'll be happy once I've bought a sailboat."

Again, thinking as a mortal, you realize the question is: What if you die without reaching your goals? How will you feel about yourself then?

When I came to terms with my expiry date I finally understood what I'm urging you to understand. *Once* is exactly how many times today comes around. You'd better make sure you're doing something that fulfills you and brings you joy each and every day. This is important, so I'll say it again.

Once is exactly how many times today comes around.

There's another danger with living for the future: What happens when you get there? In his autobiography, astronaut Buzz Aldrin said that after walking on the moon, everything else in life seemed insignificant. Aldrin was clearly a person who was so focused on one goal for so long that he forgot simply walking on this planet each day is a tremendously significant achievement.

Planning is fine. Worrying is not. The future isn't your concern until it becomes the present.

The Present

I use each moment to the fullest.

What do we miss by being too focused on the past or the future? How many little pleasures slip by us undetected?

A beautiful sunrise or sunset is lost because we're focusing on what the rush-hour traffic will do to our daily schedule.

We miss out on our children growing up because we're either dwelling on what cute newborns they once were, or we're wishing they would reach the next developmental milestone.

- We can't wait for them to start eating solid food.
- We look forward to the time they begin sleeping through the night.
- We eagerly anticipate their first words.
- The video camera is on standby for their first steps.
- We wish toilet training would go faster.
- Next comes the first day of school.
- And so on.

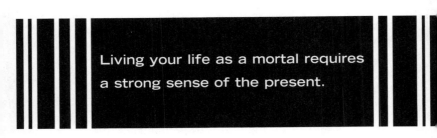

Living your life as a mortal requires a strong sense of the present.

We think of a dear friend and realize we haven't seen or spoken to him in months. We tell ourselves, "I must call him," but we just never have the time, which is ironic because *now* is the only time we ever have.

I'll say that again.

Now is the only time we ever have.

Now is the only time you can be happy.

Now is the only time you can be free.

You can only do one thing right now, and **you** get to choose what it is. Will you choose to be happy or sad? Excited or angry?

Any future you may have is a direct result of the thoughts, words and actions you choose now. Eckhart Tolle captured it wonderfully when he wrote, "The inner journey has only one step, the step you are taking right now."

There's no sense in setting a weight-loss goal without looking at the present to see what you can do to advance yourself in the right direction. The pounds aren't lost because of grandiose actions such as joining a health club or buying an expensive piece of exercise equipment for your basement. They're lost because of the decisions made at each and every mealtime, by deciding to go to the health club today or by clearing the junk off the exercise equipment and actually using it.

Living your life as a mortal requires a strong sense of the present. You must be vigilant to guard against slipping into the past or the future. Since society, for the most part, is a society of immortals, you must take care not to slip back into your old ways.

Living in the present frees you from fear. Rather than being paralyzed by asking, "What would I do if...," you can draw incredible power from saying, "What shall I do now?" The latter question is much easier to answer, since it has far fewer variables to worry about.

That's why I tattooed my expiry date on my shoulder. It serves as a daily reminder for me of how precious life really is. When I see the barcode in the shower each morning, it sets the right tone for the rest of my day.

I'm certainly not suggesting you go out and tattoo yourself, but I do recommend you keep a daily reminder of your mortality around you. That's why I've given you your own expiry date barcode at the back of the book. As I suggested, make copies and keep them where you'll see them every day.

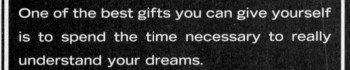

One of the best gifts you can give yourself is to spend the time necessary to really understand your dreams.

Dreams

I always strive to ensure that my every thought, word and action is moving me in the direction of my dreams.

Our hopes, dreams and aspirations are some of the most important things in our lives. Getting in touch with our deepest desires is a very critical step in understanding who we really are. One of the best gifts you can give yourself is to spend the time necessary to really understand your dreams.

The most powerful decisions we make are the decisions that move us in the direction of our dreams. If you aren't in touch with your dreams, how will you know if you're on the right track or not?

Please don't tell me you're using external feedback to help you make decisions. My experience has taught me that if you live your life according to what others say, do or think, you run the risk of waking up one day and not liking who you've become.

There's an entire section devoted to dreams in my *Mortality Manual* workbook. In that section, I provide a series of exercises to help you uncover your dreams and another series of exercises to help you live those dreams.

I find it incredibly sad when someone tells me they've just realized they've been living out someone else's plans. We've all experienced it. Work, family and social life put constant demands on our time and energy. We get caught up in other people's dramas. We find ourselves worrying about something that's someone else's priority.

I call this 'living by default' and if we're not careful, it can become a way of life. It's something that immortals do all the time. We mortals, on the other hand, realize how precious our lives are and we take the time to set our own priorities, follow our dreams and live our lives on purpose.

The most exciting part about getting in touch with your dreams is that at any given moment, you'll know exactly *why* you're doing something and you'll find great peace in the fact that you've consciously and purposely decided to do it.

How much more powerful would your life be if you were living like that?

When it comes to defining and living your dreams, there are no right or wrong answers. The only measure is:

Can you live with those answers?

More importantly, can you die with those answers?

Fear

Because fear is based on an imagined future, my focus on the present makes me fearless.

Why isn't everyone living the life of his or her dreams? If the secret formula is simply to understand your dreams and move constantly in the direction of those dreams, why isn't everyone doing it? The biggest obstacle that people face is fear.

- Fear of the unknown
- Fear of rejection
- Fear of loss
- Fear of looking foolish

Fear keeps us from moving forward towards our dreams. Fear keeps us paralyzed and immobilized.

I want to make an important distinction between fear and fright. Fright is instinctual while fear is learned. Fright is a temporary reaction to a direct stimulus; it initiates the 'fight or flight' response of the nervous system. Fright is action-oriented and based in real-time. Fear, on the other hand, is paralyzing and based in the future.

Fear (and all of its variations such as dread, despair and terror) is based on an imagined future event. This is precisely why fear leads to paralysis and kills our dreams. After all, what possible action is there against something that hasn't happened yet? How do we know the appropriate steps to take?

- You could lose your job.
- Your spouse might cheat on you.
- You may go bankrupt.
- You might be rejected.
- You could have a car accident.

In some cases, the basis for this imagined outcome is something from your past. Perhaps one of your parents was suddenly let go from a job they had held for a long time and that was considered 'very secure.'

Or perhaps there's a legitimate reason to fear the loss of your job. If your company is the target of a hostile takeover, and you know your position will be redundant in the new organization, then there's a stronger possibility your imagined future will come to pass.

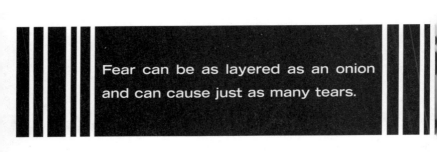

Fear can be as layered as an onion and can cause just as many tears.

But you need to realize that, ultimately, the issue isn't whether or not the imagined event will actually happen. Instead, the issue is understanding what valuable message that particular fear holds for you. Getting to the root meaning of your fear is extremely valuable in helping you overcome it.

Let's stay with the job loss example. Ask yourself what it would mean to lose your job.

Maybe the answer is that you wouldn't be able to afford to keep your house. If so, then perhaps you could use this fear to motivate you to start an aggressive savings and investment program.

Maybe the answer is that you'd have a very hard time finding another job. If so, then perhaps you could investigate night classes to upgrade your current skills, or learn a new skill or trade to help make yourself more marketable.

Or maybe you'll discover that the answer just leads to more questions. Fear can be as layered as an onion and can cause just as many tears. Begin to peel back the layers to see what lies at the true heart of the fear.

Naturally, facing your fears head-on like this is an uncomfortable task. So why do I recommend such a difficult process? Because it's important to separate those fears that carry legitimate messages from the ones that don't. Any fear that has a legitimate message also brings with it the gift of a course of action to avoid the feared outcome.

Let me re-state my definition of fear: Fear is a negative emotional state caused by thinking about an imagined future event.

In her book, *Feel The Fear And Do It Anyway*, Susan Jeffers says, "At the bottom of every one of your fears is simply the fear that you can't handle whatever life may bring you."

Personally, I'd go one level deeper. I believe that at the bottom of all fear is the fear that you can't handle the one thing life is sure to bring you: death.

Once you've acknowledged and accepted your own mortality, fear loses its power over you. After all, what's the worst that can happen to you if you've already come to terms with death?

My prescription to protect against the ravages of fear is simple: Stay out of the imagined future and live in the present. Deal with what is real.

Mindful Awareness

...the gift I give to myself – today and every day!

One of the most important things you need to understand about the Mortality Manifesto pledge is that it's an ongoing process and not something you can simply do once. You need to have a daily commitment to living your life on purpose.

Think of New Year's resolutions that you may have made in the past. If you're anything like I was, you start out with great intentions. You have some sort of mission statement such as, "I'll lose 10 pounds by spring." You also start out with a plan. Maybe you join a health club or purchase new cookbooks. I always found that my downfall wasn't in the planning or the purpose, it was the daily follow-through that got me every time.

I practice what I call 'mindful awareness.' For me, mindful awareness is simply living each moment with as much presence as possible.

I'll explain mindful awareness more clearly by contrasting it with what it isn't. Mindful awareness isn't walking around wearing black, feeling depressed or carrying a placard proclaiming, "Repent – the end is near!"

Mindful awareness isn't spending every dime you have, throwing caution to the wind, driving fast cars and bungee jumping every day. Mindful awareness is a quiet attentiveness that moves, like an undercurrent, through your everyday life.

You strive to be continually aware of your mortality.

You strive to pay attention to the gifts each moment has to offer.

You strive to tap into the power that's found by remaining present and not slipping into the past or future.

At first, you might think that accepting your own mortality is the most difficult part of my message. But once you begin by acknowledging your mortality, you'll gradually come to accept it over time.

No, the most difficult part of the Mortality Manifesto pledge is carrying your new perspective with you on a daily basis. We live in a world filled with immortals. It can be difficult to resist their messages and their mindset.

Death often seems so far away. When you're feeling perfectly fine, with no aches, no pains and no symptoms, death is the furthest thing from your mind. A hospital environment, with its wires and tubes and machines, makes it harder to ignore your mortality. But not everyone spends his or her last days in a hospital.

Mindful awareness isn't just about hanging onto your new mortal perspective. There's tremendous power to be found in practicing mindful awareness. One of my favorite authors on this subject is Eckhart Tolle. As Tolle points out, "Nothing ever happened in the past; it happened in the Now. Nothing will ever happen in the future; it will happen in the Now."

If we accept that nothing ever happens in the past or future, then it becomes very clear that the present, or right now, is the only time we can make things happen. Now is the only time that has any power, and the more we are tuned in to the now, the more powerful we are.

Ultimately, my goal in writing this book and sharing my story with you is nothing less than to get you thinking carefully about how you live your life. I want you to know the joy that comes from living a life free of fear and regret. A life lived on purpose. A life where you are at continual peace with your environment. A life of power.

That is my wish for you.

Enjoy *now*!

Enjoy *now*!

Epilogue

One of the first questions people ask me when they hear my story is, "How old are you now?"

Just in case you are one of the curious...

translates to:

031800

or March 18, 2000—the date of my 30th birthday.

Here's how my story has played out so far.

Once I had come to terms with my own mortality and realized that now is the only time that matters, I largely forgot about my expiry date. I didn't bother going back to the cardiologist or worrying about dates and timelines. I simply set about living my life on purpose.

The only time it crossed my mind was once a month when I was paying my student loan. I would laugh each time I made my payment because I was so sure the bank was never going to get all of its money.

You may recall that one of the things that disturbed me the most about being told my expiry date was the implication it held for my dream of raising a family. I'm happy to say that once I discovered the power that comes from accepting mortality, I was no longer plagued by doubts in this area. I simply began to date again.

At first, I was a bit apprehensive. My concern centered around when I should share my news with someone I was dating. Luckily, the issue usually resolved itself. My heartbeat is very loud and very distinctive, so once someone slow danced with me or hugged me close, they would often feel or hear my heart and ask why it was so loud.

I was dating one woman for a couple of years and she knew my entire story, including the expiry date. She was quite insistent that I get a second opinion from a different cardiologist. As I explained earlier, I saw no merit in doing so, but to appease her I called and made an appointment for January 19, 1996. It had been eight years since I had last seen a cardiologist.

To my complete surprise, the cardiologist they booked me to see was someone who had been my cardiologist for a number of years when I was a child. He had moved from the children's hospital to the heart institute.

I remembered him as a towering man with a thick accent and very striking features. When I met him in his office that day, he still had a thick accent and striking features but he was much less towering. As a child I found him very tall, but now that I was a 6-foot-tall adult he wasn't much taller than I was.

He shook my hand and beckoned me to sit down. On his desk was the infamous thick file. He opened it up at the first page and began to read. He skimmed the reports and diagnostic results with efficient thoroughness. Then he came to his own notes from when he had treated me as a child.

"Ah! I remember you!" he beamed. As if to prove this, he went on to tell me details of my family and what I had told him I wanted to be when I grew up.

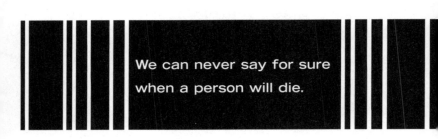

We can never say for sure
when a person will die.

Then with all seriousness he returned to the file. As he progressed through the years, his eyebrows would raise occasionally and he would periodically say, "Hmmm..." as if considering something very carefully.

When he finished, he closed the file and took a long look at me.

"Where is the pain?" he asked.

"I have no pain."

"No pain? How about shortness of breath?

"Not unless I run for a period of time."

"No pain. No shortness of breath. Then what symptoms are you having?"

"I have no symptoms. I feel fine."

"Then why are you here, my boy?"

"I'm here to get a second opinion."

I proceeded to tell him what his colleague had told me on

my last visit. I recounted the words that had been burned into my consciousness. When I finished speaking the doctor said nothing. He simply looked at me for a long time.

Then he let out a long sigh and said, "I don't know why he would have told you that. We can never say for sure when a person will die."

He went on to explain that the other doctor had based his prediction on the fact that the bottom chambers of my heart are reversed. In a normal heart, there are two lower chambers: a strong one, which sends blood to the entire body, and a weaker one, which only sends blood to the lungs. In my case, because of the reversal, the weaker chamber was taxed with supplying blood to my entire body. The first cardiologist had predicted that the tremendous amount of added strain would cause the weaker chamber to burn out before I reached 30 years of age.

"He was forgetting one crucial thing in his assessment. You have such a large hole between the two bottom chambers that they effectively operate as one," the cardiologist explained.

I wasn't sure I was hearing things correctly. It sounded extremely positive. He spent the next 15 minutes explaining the impact that each of my conditions has on my overall health and how each one seems to balance another one quite nicely. His final assessment was that, although they wanted to continue monitoring me with annual checkups, there was no reason to think I wouldn't live as long as anyone else.

I sat in stunned silence.

My expiry date had just been lifted!

You would think I'd be happy about that, wouldn't you? I was... for a time. Initially, I was overjoyed – I wasn't going to die at 30! I had my entire life ahead of me.

For a number of months I worked very hard to forget about my expiry date. After all, it didn't matter any more. It was irrelevant.

But the question that kept surfacing was, "How does this news change how I live my life?" The tendency was to go back to believing I was immortal again. And guess what?

That thought scared me even more than my expiry date.

I firmly believed (and still do) that being given an early wake-up call at age 18 was the best gift I had ever received. I was living my life on purpose and making my decisions based on lessons I had learned by embracing my mortality.

I felt I was a more powerful person because I no longer feared death. Never underestimate the incredible effect that the fear of your own death has on your decisions. Only when you're free of the fear do you realize how much control it had over you.

My concern was that if I let go of all of these lessons and slipped back into the land of the immortals, I risked losing my new-found power. So I made a conscious decision to never let these lessons get away from me. Life was just as precious and fleeting as it was before I got the revised prognosis.

In the fall of 1998, I met a wonderful woman named Heather. A year after that, she proposed to me and we were married on May 25, 2000—two months after my expiry date.

In the summer of 2001, I converted the numerals of the date of my 30th birthday into a barcode and had it tattooed on my shoulder. There, it serves as a daily reminder of the lessons I've learned.

In the fall of 2001, Heather and I became pregnant. The ultrasound test revealed it was a boy. We had a very sophisticated fetal echocardiogram conducted to ensure his heart was normal. I was so relieved to have the doctor show us the ultrasound monitor with four tiny, perfect chambers magically beating away. On August 8, 2002, Heather gave birth to our son Benjamin.

I continue to visit the cardiologist for annual checkups, and at a recent appointment the doctor told me that I continue to be a source of amazement to the staff. Now those are words to savor from your cardiologist.

There is one sad note to the story.

On January 7, 2004, I received a letter from the people at my bank informing me they had just received the final payment on my student loan. They got their money after all.

About the Author

 Patrick Mathieu is a speaker, author and coach. In his keynote speeches, workshops and seminars, Patrick shares the lessons he has learned in coming to terms with his mortality, and shows others how to use those lessons so that their own lives may be filled with vitality.

An award-winning speaker, Patrick began studying and practicing the art of public speaking in the seventh grade. He was the valedictorian of his high school's graduating class, president of his high school's award-winning debating society and a member of the prestigious McGill University Debating Union. He has also performed amateur stand-up comedy in Montreal. Patrick remains an active member of Toastmasters International.

Patrick believes very strongly in the importance of nurturing young people to become leaders for tomorrow. This conviction led him to become involved for four years with the In-School Mentoring program through the Big Brothers Big Sisters organization.

Patrick is the founding president of the Canadian Congenital Heart Alliance, a group dedicated to raising awareness about congenital heart defects (CHD) and supporting those affected by CHD.

Patrick currently lives outside of Toronto with his wife, Heather, and their young son, Benjamin.

Canadian Congenital Heart Alliance

In the spring of 2004, I became the founding president of the Canadian Congenital Heart Alliance (CCHA). Congenital heart defects (CHD) are the most common form of birth defect, affecting approximately one out of every 100 births. The CCHA was formed to provide support to Canadians affected by CHD by:

- Raising the profile of CHD in Canada
- Helping patients find a congenital heart facility or expert in their area
- Offering peer support and counseling
- Helping patients make the transition from the pediatric to adult system
- Providing educational information and resources
- Working with other CHD organizations worldwide to increase awareness and understanding

To find out more, please visit http://www.cchaonline.ca.

A portion of the proceeds from this book is donated to the CCHA.

This is your last day.

Write today's date beneath the barcode. Keep the barcode
and date with you as a daily reminder of your mortality.

_____

Ordering Books

To order additional copies of this book or to get your copy
of *The Mortality Manual: A Workbook for Tapping into the
Power of Mortality*, visit:

http://www.whatsyourexpirydate.com

Booking Patrick Mathieu

To book Patrick Mathieu for a keynote speech, workshop
or seminar, or to learn more about his coaching practice,
visit:

http://www.mathieu.com